Phonemic Awareness

Teaching Notes
with Home Connection

Grade One

Rigby®

Dear Family,

In school, I am learning the different sounds the letters of the alphabet represent. I am learning that sounds work together to make words. I am singing fun songs to help me learn these sounds.

I will be bringing copies of the songs home so I can sing them for you. We can learn to sing the songs together, too.

Many of the words in the songs begin or end with the same sound and letter. We can look at the words and you can help me read them.

When we read books together, we can look for words that begin or end with the same sound and letter. We can even hunt for words in books and newspapers or on signs in stores or in our neighborhood. We can read the words together.

Singing the song with me or hunting for words in books and on signs are fun ways to help me learn how to read. Knowing the sounds in a word will also help me learn how to spell. Let's sing together!

Your child,

Table of Contents

What Is Phonemic Awareness?

The smallest, individual speech sounds that make up a word are called phonemes. Phonemic awareness is the ability to hear, identify, and manipulate the phonemes in spoken words. Phonemic awareness skills can help children learn to read, spell, and write.

Phonemic awareness is one part of phonological awareness. Phonemic awareness skills concentrate on hearing and identifying spoken language sounds. Children must be aware of how these sounds are put together to make up words before they can become successful readers. Children who know how to manipulate the sounds of spoken words can then relate the phonemes to the graphemes in written language.

How to Teach Phonemic Awareness Effectively

For phonemic awareness instruction to be effective, children must be taught to hear, identify, and manipulate sounds in spoken language. Many different activities can be used to teach phonemic awareness. Children can be asked to

- **isolate** phonemes by recognizing individual sounds in words.
- **identify** phonemes by recognizing the same sound in different words.
- **categorize** phonemes by recognizing one word in a group of words that begins with a different sound.
- **blend** phonemes by combining a sequence of separately spoken sounds to form a word.
- **segment** phonemes by breaking a word into its separate sounds.
- **delete** phonemes from a word to make a new word.
- **add** phonemes to a word to make a new word.
- **substitute** one phoneme in a word for another to make a new word.

Phonemic awareness instruction can benefit all children who are learning to read. The ability to hear and identify phonemes is a valuable pre-reading tool. Phonemic awareness instruction, especially the teaching of how to segment words into phonemes, can also help improve children's spelling skills.

How to Use the Phonemic Awareness Posters

The *Word Works* Phonemic Awareness strand uses songs to teach sound recognition in words. Each of the 32 write-on, wipe-off posters features a song based on a familiar tune that includes rhyme, rhythm, and repetition. Each song teaches a phoneme as well as the letter that represents the sound. A companion audio CD can be played while children hum or sing along. On the back of each poster is a simple three-step lesson plan to accompany the song. The lesson includes

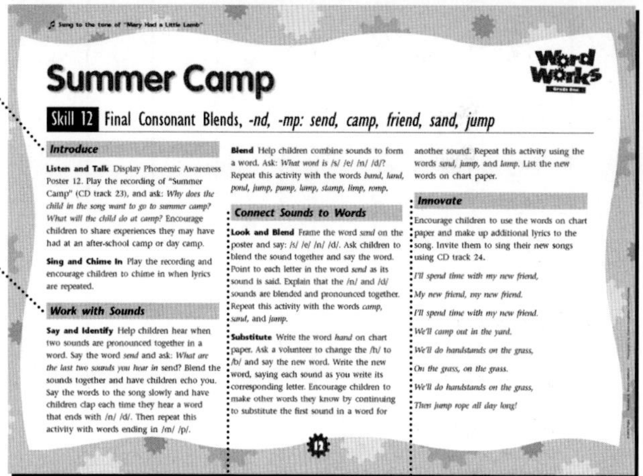

Sung to the tune of "Mary Had a Little Lamb"

Summer Camp

Word Works

Skill 12 Final Consonant Blends, *-nd, -mp: send, camp, friend, sand, jump*

Introduce

Listen and Talk Display Phonemic Awareness Poster 12. Play the recording of "Summer Camp" (CD track 23), and ask: *Why does the child in the song want to go to summer camp? What will the child do at camp?* Encourage children to share experiences they may have had at an after-school camp or day camp.

Sing and Chime In Play the recording and encourage children to chime in when lyrics are repeated.

Work with Sounds

Say and Identify Help children hear when two sounds are pronounced together in a word. Say the word *send* and ask: *What are the last two sounds you hear in* send? Blend the sounds together and have children echo you. Say the words to the song slowly and have children clap each time they hear a word that ends with /n/ /d/. Then repeat this activity with words ending in /m/ /p/.

Blend Help children combine sounds to form a word. Ask: *What word is /s/ /e/ /n/ /d/?* Repeat this activity with the words *band, land, pond, jump, pump, lamp, stamp, limp, romp.*

Connect Sounds to Words

Look and Blend Frame the word *send* on the poster and say: /s/ /e/ /n/ /d/. Ask children to blend the sound together and say the word. Point to each letter in the word *send* as its sound is said. Explain that the /n/ and /d/ sounds are blended and pronounced together. Repeat this activity with the words *camp, sand,* and *jump.*

Substitute Write the word *hand* on chart paper. Ask a volunteer to change the /h/ to /b/ and say the new word. Write the new word, saying each sound as you write its corresponding letter. Encourage children to make other words they know by continuing to substitute the first sound in a word for another sound. Repeat this activity using the words *send, jump,* and *lamp.* List the new words on chart paper.

Innovate

Encourage children to use the words on chart paper and make up additional lyrics to the song. Invite them to sing their new songs using CD track 24.

I'll spend time with my new friend,
My new friend, my new friend.
I'll spend time with my new friend.
We'll camp out in the yard.
We'll do handstands on the grass,
On the grass, on the grass.
We'll do handstands on the grass,
Then jump rope all day long!

12

- **Introduce** Children will listen to, talk about, sing, and act out the lyrics to the song.
- **Work with Sounds** Children will isolate and identify individual sounds in words by engaging in a variety of phonemic awareness activities.
- **Connect Sounds to Words** Children will engage in different activities to connect phonemes to the letters of the alphabet and will relate phonemic awareness to reading and writing.
- **Innovate** or **Extend** Many of the lessons include an Innovate section which encourages children to create their own lyrics to the poster song. Children can sing their new songs to the accompaniment of an instrumental CD track. Other lessons include an Extend section which provides additional activities for reinforcing the lesson skills.

Make a Home Connection

Every lesson includes a reduced-size reproducible poster with a Home Connection activity written at the bottom of the poster. The poster can be sent home with each child after the class lesson is completed. The reproducible posters can be found in this Teaching Notes book. There is also a reproducible Family Letter on page two of this book that is designed to be sent home with the first poster. Encourage children to sing the songs with their families and to share what they have learned with family members.

Phonemic Awareness Instruction Chart

Phonemic awareness and phoneme manipulation skills can be taught using a variety of activities. Each lesson in the *Word Works* Phonemic Awareness strand uses several activities to teach children how to hear, identify, and manipulate phonemes.

Phonemic Awareness Instruction Activities

Skill	Poster Name	Isolate	Identify	Categorize	Blend	Segment	Delete	Add	Substitute
1	Dad, Max, and Dan	x	x	x	x			x	x
2	What Did My Kitten Do?	x	x	x	x			x	x
3	My Job	x	x	x	x			x	x
4	My Pup	x	x	x	x			x	x
5	My Red Hen, Nell	x	x	x	x			x	x
6	Watch the Dog!	x	x		x	x			
7	A Duck Named Jack	x	x		x	x			
8	Clap Your Hands	x	x		x	x		x	
9	Frogs	x	x		x	x	x	x	
10	Swim, Snack, and Skip	x	x		x	x	x	x	
11	Frank and Hank Must Study!	x	x		x	x	x		
12	Summer Camp	x	x		x	x			x
13	Jane and I Skate	x	x					x	x
14	To Grandma's House	x	x			x			x
15	I Will Ride My Bike	x	x					x	x
16	My Pizza Pie	x	x			x			

Skill	Poster Name	Isolate	Identify	Categorize	Blend	Segment	Delete	Add	Substitute
17	I Saw a Mole!	x	x					x	x
18	We See a Toad!	x	x			x			
19	My Book Is So Good!	x	x		x				x
20	June Plays a Tune	x	x	x				x	x
21	I'm as Happy as Can Be!	x	x	x		x			
22	The Best Team!	x	x		x	x		x	x
23	Bucky, My Pup	x	x	x					
24	Shane Got Sea Shells!	x	x			x			x
25	Theo's Tooth	x	x			x			x
26	I See a Gray Whale	x	x			x			x
27	Chowder for Lunch!	x	x			x	x		
28	Norm and Marge	x	x					x	x
29	I Spy	x	x		x	x			
30	Roy and Joy's Party	x	x			x			x
31	Count the Clouds	x	x			x	x	x	x
32	I Saw Paul	x	x			x			x

Dad, Max, and Dan

Dad cooked ham and eggs
In his new pan.
Max helped out, too,
And so did Dan.
After breakfast Dan took
His long nap.
Sam, the cat, slept on his lap!

Home Connection Your child is reviewing words that include the **short a** sound. Encourage him or her to sing "Dad, Max, and Dan" with you. When you are reading a favorite book together, point out words that end in –**ad**, –**am**, –**an**, –**ax**, –**ap**, and –**at**. Help your child read the words.

Dad, Max, and Dan

Skill 1 Short *a* Word Family Review *(-ad, -am, -an, -ax, -ap, -at): Dad, ham, pan, Max, Dan, nap, Sam, cat, lap*

Introduce

Listen and Share Display Phonemic Awareness Poster 1 and play the recording of "Dad, Max, and Dan" (CD track 1). Ask: *What did Dad do? How did Max and Dan help Dad? What did Dan do after breakfast?* Ask children if they ever help make breakfast, set the table, or help clean up after meals. Encourage volunteers to share their experiences with the class.

Work with Sounds

Review, Identify, and Categorize Ask children to say the middle sound they hear in the words *Dad* and *ham*. Say /a/-/a/-/a/ and have them echo you. Then say the words to the song slowly and have children raise their hands each time they hear a word with short *a* as the middle sound. If children raise their hands on *and* and *after,* reassure them that they did hear the short *a* sound, but it was at the beginning of the word. Then, have children identify the word in a set of three words that has a different middle sound. Say: *Which word doesn't belong:* cat, man, hop? Repeat this activity with other groups of words, such as *hen/cap/mat; pan/dot/Sam; tag/lap/fin.*

Blend Help children blend sounds together to form a word. Say: *What word is* /h/ /a/ /t/? Repeat this activity by using other words from short *a* word families, such as *bag, jam, van, cat,* and *lap.*

Substitute Have children make rhyming words by substituting the first sound in a word with another sound they know. Say: *My word is* ham. *Change* /h/ *to* /j/. *What's the new word?* Encourage children to choose other sounds to substitute for /j/ and to say the new words. Repeat this activity with *Dad, pan,* and *cat.*

Connect Sounds to Words

Add and Write On chart paper, write the word families *–ad, –am –an, –ax, –ap,* and *–at.* Frame and say *–ad.* Have children echo you. Ask volunteers to add sounds they know to the beginning of *–ad* to make new words. Write the words under *–ad,* saying the sounds separately as you write the corresponding letters. Have children echo you and blend the sounds together to say the words. Repeat this activity for other short *a* word families.

Sing and Clap Play the recording, tracking the print as the class sings. Ask children to clap on words with the short *a* sound.

Extend

Invite children to make up sentences using one or more of the words written on chart paper. Write the sentences on chart paper and read them together.

♫ **Sung to the tune of "I've Been Working on the Railroad"**

What Did My Kitten Do?

Did my kitten rip the blanket?
Did she dig a hole?
Did my kitten snap a big twig
And sip milk from a bowl?
Did my kitten tip the flowers
On the window sill?
If she did, Mom will be angry.
I know that she will!

Home Connection Your child is reviewing words that include the **short i** sound. Encourage him or her to sing "What Did My Kitten Do?" with you. When you are reading the newspaper, point out words that end in **–id**, **–ip**, **–ig**, and **–ill**. Help your child read the words.

What Did My Kitten Do?

Word Works Grade One

Skill 2 Short *i* Word Family Review *(-id, -ip, -ig, -ill): did, rip, dig, big, twig, sip, tip, sill, will*

Introduce

Listen, Ask, and Support Display Phonemic Awareness Poster 2 and play the recording of "What Did My Kitten Do?" (CD track 3). Then, repeat a question asked in the song and ask children for the answer. Have a volunteer support the answer by finding evidence on the poster.

Act Out Invite children to make up actions to the song. For example: Have children pretend they are ripping a blanket on the word *rip* and digging a hole on the word *dig*. Play the song again and encourage children to sing along while acting out the lyrics.

Work with Sounds

Review and Identify Ask children to say the middle sound they hear in the words *did* and *rip*. Say /i/-/i/-/i/ and have them echo you. Then say the words to the song slowly and have children raise their hands each time they hear a word with short *i* as the middle sound. Children may raise their hands on *kitten, milk,* and *window* along with the words in the short *i* word families.

Categorize Have children identify the word in a set of three words that has a different middle sound. Say: *Which word doesn't belong:* rip, snap, dig? Repeat this activity with other groups of words, such as *big/cap/sit; tip/bill/tag; cat/lip/fin.*

Substitute Have children make rhyming words by substituting the first sound in a word with another sound they know. Say: *My word is* did. *Change* /d/ *to* /h/. *What's the new word?* Encourage children to choose other sounds to substitute for /h/ and to say the new words. Repeat this activity with *rip, dig,* and *sill.*

Connect Sounds to Words

Add and Write On chart paper, write the word families *–id, –ip, –ig, –it,* and *–ill.* Frame and say *–id*. Have children echo you. Ask volunteers to add sounds they know to the beginning of *–id* to make new words. Write the words under *–id,* saying the sounds separately as you write the corresponding letters. Have children echo you and blend the sounds together to say the words. Repeat this activity for other short *i* word families.

Sing and Tap Play the recording, tracking the print as the class sings. Ask children to tap their lips on words with the short *i* sound.

Extend

Invite children to make up sentences using one or more of the words written on chart paper. Write the sentences on chart paper and read them together.

My Job

Sometimes it is my job
To walk our dog, Dot.
Sometimes it is my job
To scrub the big pot.

Sometimes it is my job
To wash with the mop.
Sometimes it is my job
To help my mom shop.

I like when I work hard
At each job I do.
I like when I help out.
I'll play when I'm through!

Home Connection Your child is reviewing words that include the **short o** sound. Encourage him or her to sing "My Job" with you. When you are reading a favorite book together, point out words that end in **–ob**, **–ot**, **–op**, and **–om**. Help your child read the words.

My Job

Word Works Grade One

Skill 3 Short *o* Word Family Review *(-ob, -ot, -op, -om): job, Dot, pot, mop, mom, shop*

Introduce

Listen and Talk Display Phonemic Awareness Poster 3. Play the recording of "My Job" (CD track 5), and ask: *What jobs does the child in the song like to do? What does the child do after helping out?* Invite children to talk about the jobs they do at home to help out. Encourage them to share their experiences.

Chime In and Act Out Play the recording and encourage children to chime in when they can. To help children learn the lyrics, create actions for the jobs mentioned in the song. For example, have them pretend they are walking a dog on the word *walk* and scrubbing a pot on the word *scrub.*

Work with Sounds

Review and Identify Ask children to say the middle sound they hear in the words *job* and *pot.* Say /o/-/o/-/o/ and have them echo you. Then say the words to the song slowly and have children raise their hands each time they hear a word with short *o* as the middle sound. While children may raise their hands on *dog,* this word does not have a true short *o* sound.

Categorize Have children identify the word in a set of three words that has a different middle sound. Say: *Which word doesn't belong:* job, cat, hot? Repeat this activity with other groups of words, such as *cob/cap/hop; pot/shop/tip; twig/not/mom.*

Substitute Have children make rhyming words by substituting the first sound in a word with another sound they know. Say: *My word is* Dot. *Change* /d/ *to* /h/. *What's the new word?* Encourage children to choose other sounds to substitute for /h/ and to say the new words. Repeat this activity with *job, mop, mom.*

Connect Sounds to Words

Add and Write On chart paper, write the word families *–ob, –ot, –op,* and *–om.* Frame and say *–ob.* Have children echo you. Ask volunteers to add sounds they know to the beginning of *–ob* to make new words. Write the words under *–ob,* saying the sounds separately as you write the corresponding letters. Have children echo you and blend the sounds together to say the words. Repeat this activity for other short *o* word families.

Find and Circle Ask volunteers to find and circle words from short *o* word families on the poster. Encourage children to say the words that they circle.

Sing and Hop Play the recording of "My Job," tracking the print from left to right as the class sings the song. Ask children to hop in place once on words that have the short *o* sound.

3

♫ **Sung to the tune of "Camptown Races"**

My Pup

My pup likes to chase the bug.
What fun! What fun!
My pup likes to chase the bug,
And run in the sun!
Pup just wants to play.
Pup plays every day.
My pup likes to chase the bug,
And run in the sun!

Home Connection Your child is reviewing words that include the **short u** sound. Encourage him or her to sing "My Pup" with you. When you are reading a favorite book together, point out words that end in –**up**, –**ug**, and –**un**.

My Pup

Word Works Grade One

Skill 4 Short *u* Word Family Review *(-up, -ug, -un): pup, bug, fun, run, sun*

Introduce

Listen and Talk Display Phonemic Awareness Poster 4. Play the recording of "My Pup" (CD track 7), and then talk about the song. Ask children what the pup likes to do. Encourage children to share stories about what their pets like to do.

Echo and Sing Say each line of the song and ask children to echo you. Then, sing the song together, encouraging children to chime in when they can. To help children learn the lyrics, point to a picture on the poster as you sing about it in the song.

Work with Sounds

Review and Identify Ask children to say the middle sound they hear in the words *pup* and *bug*. Say /u/-/u/-/u/ and have them echo you. Then say the words to the song slowly and have children raise their hands each time they hear a word with short *u* as the middle sound.

Categorize Have children identify the word in a set of three words that has a different middle sound. Say: *Which word doesn't belong:* pup, pat, fun? Repeat this activity with other groups of words, such as *up/tap/rug; cup/run/top; tug/hot/bun.*

Substitute Have children make rhyming words by substituting the first sound in a word with another sound they know. Say: *My word is* bug. *Change* /b/ *to* /r/. *What's the new word?* Encourage children to choose other sounds to substitute for /r/ and to say the new word. Repeat this activity with *pup* and *run.*

Connect Sounds to Words

Add and Write On chart paper, write the word families *–un, –ug,* and *–up.* Frame and say *–un.* Have children echo you. Ask volunteers to add sounds they know to the beginning of *–un* to make new words. Write the words under *–un,* saying the sounds separately as you write the corresponding letters. Have children echo you and blend the sounds together to say the words. Repeat this activity for the other short *u* word families

Find and Circle Ask volunteers to find and circle words from short *u* word families on the poster. Encourage children to say the words that they circle.

Sing and Clap Play the recording of "My Pup," tracking the print from left to right as the class sings the song. Ask children to jump up on words that have the short *u* sound.

Extend

Invite children to make up sentences using one or more of the words written on chart paper. Write the sentences on chart paper. Then track the print as the class reads the sentences together.

4

♫ **Sung to the tune of "Rockabye, Baby"**

My Red Hen, Nell

I have a red hen.
Her name is Nell.
When Nell is hungry,
She rings her bell.
I hear the bell,
Then go to the shed.
That's where I get Nell's food.
She'll be well fed!

5

Home Connection Your child is reviewing words that include the **short e** sound. Encourage him or her to sing "My Red Hen, Nell" with you. When you go to the grocery store, look for words on food labels that end in **–ed**, **–en**, **–ell**, or **–et**. Help your child read the words.

Word Works Grade One

My Red Hen, Nell

Skill 5 Short *e* Word Family Review *(-ed, -en, -ell, -et): red, hen, Nell, bell, then, shed, get, well, fed*

Introduce

Listen and Talk Display Phonemic Awareness Poster 5. Play the recording of "My Red Hen, Nell" (CD track 9), and talk about the song. Ask children: *Who is Nell? What does Nell do when she's hungry?* Discuss with children the responsibilities involved in caring for an animal.

Echo and Sing Say each line of the song and ask children to echo you. Then, sing the song together with the recording, encouraging children to chime in when they can. Ask a volunteer to ring a bell when the word *bell* is sung.

Work with Sounds

Review and Identify Ask children to say the middle sound they hear in the words *red* and *hen*. Say /e/-/e/-/e/ and have them echo you. Then say the words to the song slowly and have children clap each time they hear a word with short *e* as the middle sound.

Categorize Have children identify the word in a set of three words that has a different middle sound. Say: *Which word doesn't belong:* den, hop, bed? Repeat this activity with other groups of words, such as *set/cup/Ted; well/hip/ten; pot/red/sell.*

Substitute Have children make rhyming words by substituting the first sound in a word with another sound they know. Say: *My word is* red. *Change* /r/ *to* /b/. *What's the new word?* Encourage children to choose other sounds to substitute for /b/ and to say the new words. Repeat this activity with *hen, bell,* and *get.*

Connect Sounds to Words

Add and Write On chart paper, write the word families *–ed, –en, –ell,* and *–et.* Frame and say *–ed*. Have children echo you. Ask volunteers to add sounds they know to the beginning of *–ed* to make new words. Write the words under *–ed,* saying the sounds separately as you write the corresponding letters. Have children echo you and blend the sounds together to say the words. If a child offers the words *head* and *said,* explain that the sounds they hear as /e/-/d/ are made by a different sequence of letters. Repeat this activity for the other short *e* word families.

Find and Circle Ask volunteers to find, circle, and say words from short *e* word families on the poster. Then, play the recording, tracking the print from left to right as the class sings.

Extend

Invite children to make up sentences using one or more of the words written on chart paper. Write the sentences on chart paper and read them together.

5

♫ Sung to the tune of "Are You Sleeping, Brother John?"

Watch the Dog!

Watch the dog run.
Watch the dog run.
He has fun. He has fun.
Watch the dog get wet now.
Watch the dog get wet now,
In the lake, in the lake.

Watch the dog dig.
Watch the dog dig,
By the log, by the log.
Watch the dog play tug now.
Watch the dog play tug now.
Watch him nap! Watch him nap!

Home Connection Your child is reviewing words that include short vowel sounds, such as **has**, **wet**, **dig**, **hot**, and **tug**. Encourage him or her to sing "Watch the Dog!" with you. When you are reading signs in your neighborhood, point out words that include these sounds. Help your child read the words.

Sung to the tune of "Are You Sleeping, Brother John?"

Watch the Dog!

Word Works Grade One

Skill 6 Short Vowel Word Family Review: *run, has, fun, get, wet, in, dig, tug, him, nap*

Introduce

Listen and Share Display Phonemic Awareness Poster 6 and play the recording of "Watch the Dog!" (CD track 11). Discuss the different things the dog does. Invite volunteers to point to pictures on the poster and explain what the dog is doing.

Sing and Act Out Say each line of the song and ask children to echo you. Play the recording again and invite children to sing along when they feel comfortable. Choose volunteers to act out the different actions in the song as they are mentioned.

Work with Sounds

Play It Again Review the sounds the short vowels make. Say /a/ and have a volunteer say a word they know or a word they heard in the song that has the short *a* sound. Repeat this activity for /e/, /i/, /o/, and /u/.

Blend Help children combine sounds to form a word. Say: *What word is* /r/ /u/ /n/? Have children repeat the individual sounds and then blend the sounds together before saying the word. Repeat this activity using words in the song from the short vowel word families.

Connect Sounds to Words

Find and Write On chart paper, write the vowels: *a, e, i, o, u.* Review the song again, tracking the print from left to right. Invite volunteers to find and circle words from the short vowel word families on the poster. Write each word on the chart paper, under the corresponding vowel. If a child circles *dog* or *log,* explain that the *o* in these words has the sound of /ȯ/ as in saw. Have volunteers offer short *o* words that they know, such as *hot* or *mop.*

Segment Return to the words on the chart paper. Have a volunteer pick a word and separate it into its individual sounds. Have the class tap out or count the sounds as they are said. Then have the class blend the individual sounds together and read the word.

Sing and Clap Play the recording of "Watch the Dog!" Track the print from left to right as children sing along. Encourage children to clap on words that have a short vowel.

Innovate

Review other short vowel words by inviting children to make up their own lyrics to the song. Have children sing their new songs, using CD track 12.

Watch my pet sit.

Watch my pet sit

On my hat, on my hat.

Watch him nap on my hat.

Watch him nap on my hat

In the sun, in the sun.

6

A Duck Named Jack

I have a duck named Jack.
His tail is white and black.
Jack will swim out to a rock,
Then quack and come right back!

And when it's twelve o'clock,
I put on my sunblock.
I swim with Jack all afternoon,
Then dry off on the dock!

Home Connection Your child is learning that the letters **ck** together stand for the **k** sound. Encourage him or her to sing "A Duck Named Jack" with you. Look through the newspaper and help your child hunt for words ending in **ck**. Say the words together.

A Duck Named Jack

Word Works Grade One

Skill 7 Words Ending with /k/ -*ck*:

duck, Jack, black, rock, quack, back, o'clock, sunblock, dock

Introduce

Listen and Share Display Phonemic Awareness Poster 7 and play the recording of "A Duck Named Jack" (CD track 13). Ask: *Who is Jack? What color is Jack's tail? Where does Jack swim? What does the child do at twelve o'clock?* Encourage children to share what they like to do with their pets or experiences they have had swimming with their families.

Work with Sounds

Say and Identify Say /k/-/k/-/k/ and have children echo you. Ask: *What is the last sound in* duck *and* Jack? Slowly repeat the lyrics to the song and have children quack like a duck each time they hear a word that ends with /k/.

Blend and Segment Help children combine sounds to form a word. Say: *What word is* /d/ /u/ /k/? Review blending sounds together using other words that end in /k/, such as *pick, sack, rock,* and *luck*. Extend the activity by helping children segment a word into its individual sounds. Ask a volunteer: *How many sounds are in* sock? *(3) Separate the sounds.* Have children tap out or count each sound as it is said. Have volunteers segment other words, such as *Jack, pack, lock, sick*.

Connect Sounds to Words

Find and Segment Frame the word *Duck* in the poster's title. Segment the sounds heard in the word: /d/ /u/ /k/. As you say each sound, point to the letter that stands for the sound. Explain to children that the letters *ck* together stand for the sound /k/. Point to *ck* and say /k/-/k/-/k/. Have children echo you. Invite volunteers to underline words on the poster that end in *ck*. Encourage them to say the words and then break the words into their separate sounds. Have children point to the letters that stand for the sounds they say.

Sing and Clap As children sing the song, track the print from left to right. Have children clap each time they see a word that ends with *ck*.

Extend

Tell Me a Story Have children make up a story using words in the song and other words they know that end with the /k/ sound spelled *ck* or *k*. Give a sentence starter to help initiate ideas. For example: *Once upon a time, a boy named Jack had a duck.* Write children's sentences on chart paper and then help the class read the story together.

7

Clap Your Hands

Clap, clap, clap your hands.
Wave a flag today.
I'm so glad we celebrate
On this special day!

8

Home Connection Your child is learning to blend the sound the letter **l** makes with other letter sounds. Encourage him or her to sing "Clap Your Hands" with you. When you're reading a favorite book, invite your child to hunt for words that begin with **bl**, **cl**, **fl**, **gl**, **pl**, and **sl**. Read the words together.

Word Works Grade One

Clap Your Hands

Skill 8 Initial Consonant Blends with *l: clap, flag, glad*

Introduce the Song

Listen and Share Display Phonemic Awareness Poster 8 and play the recording of "Clap Your Hands" (CD track 15). Ask: *What are the people in the picture celebrating? How are the people celebrating?* Encourage children to share how they celebrate special events.

Sing, Act Out, and March Play the recording and encourage children to chime in when they are able. Invite them to act out the song. They can clap at the beginning of the song and then pretend to wave a flag. Have a volunteer lead classmates in a line around the room, marching in time to the music.

Work with Sounds

Say, Clap, and Identify Help children hear when two sounds are pronounced together in a word. Ask: *What are the first two sounds in* clap? Blend the sounds together and have children echo you. Ask them to clap each time they hear a word that begins with /k/ /l/. Say: *climb, clock, club, jump, pat, clarinet, click, fan, clown.* Repeat this activity with other initial consonant blends with *l: bl (black, block, blue), fl (flag, flutter, flip), gl (glitter, glue, glove), pl (place, plum, plant), and sl (slip, slow, slime).*

Blend Have children combine sounds to form a word. Say: *What word is /k/ /l/ /a/ /p/?* Repeat this activity with the words *glad, slip, plop, clip,* and *black.*

Segment Have children segment a word into its individual sounds. Ask a volunteer: *How many sounds are in* flag? *(4)* Invite the volunteer to say each sound as the class taps out or counts them. Repeat this activity with the words *block, clap, flat, plan,* and *slap.*

Connect Sounds to Words

Look and Blend Frame the word *flag* and say: /f/ /l/ /a/ /g/. Ask children to blend the sounds together and say the word. Point to each letter in the word *flag* as its sound is said. Explain that the /f/ and /l/ sounds are blended and pronounced together. Repeat this activity with the words *clap* and *glad.*

Make a New Word Use magnetic letters to write the word *pan.* Say the sound each letter stands for as you place the letters on a cookie sheet. Have children repeat the individual sounds and then blend them together to say *pan.* Ask: *How many sounds are in* pan? *(3)* Then add an *l* to *pan* to make *plan* and ask a volunteer to say each sound in the new word. Ask: *What is the new word? How many sounds are in* plan? *(4)* Repeat this activity with the words *sip/slip; lap/clap; lad/glad.* Point out the initial consonant blends with *l* and remind children that these sounds are pronounced together.

8

Frogs

I draw three frogs
Hopping in the green grass.
They are friendly
Grinning right at me!

Home Connection Your child is learning to blend the sound the letter **r** makes with other letter sounds. Encourage him or her to sing "Frogs" with you. When you're in the grocery store, invite your child to hunt for words that begin with **br**, **cr**, **dr**, **fr**, **gr**, **pr**, and **tr**. Read the words together.

Frogs

Word Works Grade One

Skill 9 Initial Consonant Blends with *r: draw, frogs, green, grass, friendly, grinning*

Introduce

Listen and Share Display Phonemic Awareness Poster 9 and play the recording of "Frogs" (CD track 17). Ask children how many frogs the child will draw in his picture. Encourage children to share experiences they may have had with frogs or possible reasons why the frogs are grinning.

Sing and Hop Play the recording and encourage children to sing along when they feel comfortable with the lyrics. Invite children to hop like frogs and grin as the music plays.

Work with Sounds

Say, Hop, and Identify Help children hear when two sounds are pronounced together in a word. Say the word *frogs* and ask: *What are the first two sounds you hear in* frogs? Blend the sounds together and have children echo you. Ask them to hop in place each time they hear a word that begins with /f/ /r/. Say: *friend, free, fan, rose, from, frilly, hot, freeze, cook,* and *fry.* Repeat this activity with other initial consonant blends with *r: br (broom, brown, broccoli); cr (crow, cream, crumb); dr (draw, dream, drive); gr (great, green, gravy); pr (pretty, princess, principal);* and *tr (tree, track, trick).*

Blend Have children combine sounds to form a word. Say: *What word is* /g/ /r/ /a/ /s/? Help children pronounce /g/ and /r/ together as a blend. Repeat this activity with the words *grin, frog, brain, drip, crop, prom,* and *truck.*

Connect Sounds to Words

Look and Segment Say the words to the song, tracking the print from left to right. As you come to a word with an initial consonant blend with *r,* underline it. Return to the underlined words and guide children in breaking each word into its separate sounds. Circle the initial consonant blends and say the two sounds together, having children echo you.

Add or Delete and Make a New Word Use magnetic letters to write the word *rip.* Say the sound each letter stands for as you place the letters on a cookie sheet. Have children repeat the individual sounds and then blend them together to say *rip.* Ask: *How many sounds are in* rip? Then add a *d* to *rip* to make *drip* and ask a volunteer to say each sound in the new word. Ask: *What is the new word? How many sounds are in* drip? Repeat this activity with the words *rip/trip; rib/crib; rag/brag; rack/crack.* Extend the activity by starting with the words that begin with blends and deleting the first letter to form a new word.

Innovate

Have children brainstorm a list of words with initial consonant blends with *r.* Invite them to make up new lyrics and sing their songs using CD track 18. For example: *I draw two crabs; Crawling in the green grass; I will help them; Crawl back to the sea!*

9

Swim, Snack, and Skip

The swans in the lake will swim, swim, swim,
Swim, swim, swim, swim, swim, swim.
The swans in the lake will swim, swim, swim.
Swans like to swim!

The sparrows in the trees will snack, snack, snack,
Snack, snack, snack, snack, snack, snack.
The sparrows in the trees will snack, snack, snack.
Sparrows like to snack!

The children in the park will skip, skip, skip,
Skip, skip, skip, skip, skip, skip.
The children in the park will skip, skip, skip.
Children like to skip!

10

Home Connection Your child is learning to blend the sound the letter **s** makes with other letter sounds. Encourage him or her to sing "Swim, Snack, and Skip" with you. When you're reading a favorite book, invite your child to hunt for words that begin with **sk**, **sl**, **sm**, **sn**, **sp**, and **sw**. Read the words together.

Swim, Snack, and Skip

Word Works Grade One

Skill 10 Initial Consonant Blends with *s: swans, swim, sparrows, snack, skip*

Introduce

Listen and Talk Display Phonemic Awareness Poster 10. Play the recording of "Swim, Snack, and Skip" (CD track 19), and ask: *What do the swans do? What do the sparrows do? What do the children do?* Encourage children to discuss what other animals like to do.

Sing and Act Out Play the recording and encourage children to chime in on the repetitive words. Invite them to act out the action words *swim, snack,* and *skip.*

Work with Sounds

Identify and Blend Help children hear when two sounds are pronounced together in a word. Say the word *swim* and ask: *What are the first two sounds you hear in* swim? Blend the sounds together and have children echo you. Ask them to pretend to swim like a swan each time they hear a word that begins with /s/ /w/. Say: *sip, swing, grass, sweet, rose, foot, swirl, sweat, cold, swap.* Repeat this activity with other initial consonant blends with /s/: *sp (spoon, spike, sponge); sn (snake, snap, snuggle); sk (skate, sky, skip); sl (sleep, sleigh, slice);* and *sm (smart, small, smock).*

Add and Delete Help children make new words by adding /s/ to existing words. Ask: *What word do you have if you add /s/ to the beginning of* top? Repeat this activity with the word pairs *nap/snap; kid/skid; lip/slip; led/sled; tack/stack; tick/stick; tub/stub; mall/small; pin/spin; pot/spot.* Extend this activity by saying the words that begin with blends and having children delete the /s/ to make a new word.

Connect Sounds to Words

Look and Segment Say the words to the song, tracking the print from left to right. As you come to a word with an initial consonant blend with *s,* underline it. Return to the underlined words and guide children in breaking each word into its separate sounds. As each sound is said, point to its corresponding letter. Circle the initial consonant blends and say the two sounds together, having children echo you.

Blend and Write Help children combine separately spoken sounds to spell a word. Ask: *What word is* /s/ /w/ /i/ /m/? Repeat the individual sounds and write the letters that represent each sound. Read the word and have children echo you. Repeat this activity with the words *skip, snap, slip, slap,* and *slit.*

Innovate

Have the class brainstorm a list of words with initial consonant blends beginning with *s.* Encourage children to make new lyrics to the song and sing their songs using CD track 20. Possible starter sentences include: *The monkeys in the tree will swing, swing, swing; The people in the store will spend, spend, spend; The skaters in the rink will spin, spin, spin.*

10

Frank and Hank Must Study!

Frank and Hank must study
For their spelling test.
They ask me to help them
Do their very best.
They learn five words on their list.
I am happy to assist.
Then we take a break before they learn the rest!

Home Connection Your child is learning to blend the sounds the letters **–nk**, **–sk**, and **–st** make at the end of a word. Encourage him or her to sing "Frank and Hank Must Study!" with you. When you're reading a newspaper, invite your child to hunt for words that end with these letters. Read the words together.

♪ Sung to the tune of "If You're Happy"

Frank and Hank Must Study!

Word Works Grade One

Skill 11 Final Consonant Blends, *-nk, -sk, -st:*

Frank, Hank, must, test, ask, best, list, assist, rest

Introduce

Listen and Talk Display Phonemic Awareness Poster 11. Play the recording of "Frank and Hank Must Study!" (CD track 21). Ask: *What are the boys doing? What do they do after they learn how to spell five words?* Encourage children to share ways they study and to talk about the study skills that work best for them.

Work with Sounds

Identify and Blend Help children hear when two sounds are pronounced together in a word. Say the word *Frank* and ask: *What are the last two sounds you hear in* Frank? Blend the sounds together and have children echo you. Ask them to clap each time they hear a word that ends with /n/ /k/. Say: *Frank, sink, Hank, Fran, wink, bank, tick, pink.* Repeat this activity with the final consonant blends *–sk (ask, risk, desk, tusk)* and *–st (test, cast, list, just).*

Delete and Make a Word Help children recognize the word that remains when a sound is removed from another word. Ask: *What is* pink *without* /k/? Repeat this activity with the words *Frank/Fran; wink/win; bank/ban; rank/ran.*

Connect Sounds to Words

Look and Segment Say the words to the song, tracking the print from left to right. As you come to a word with a final consonant blend of *–nk, –sk,* or *–st,* underline it. Return to the underlined words and guide children in breaking each word into its separate sounds. As each sound is said, point to its corresponding letter. Circle the final consonant blends and say the two sounds together, having children echo you.

Blend and Write Help children combine separately spoken sounds to spell a word. Ask: *What word is* /t/ /e/ /s/ /t/? Repeat the individual sounds and write the letters that represent each sound: /t/, write *t;* /e/, write *e;* /s/, write *s;* /t/, write *t.* Read the word and have children echo you. Repeat this activity with the words *best, list, Frank, wink, task,* and *disk.* Have volunteers match the individual sounds they hear to letters of the alphabet to spell the words.

Extend

Brainstorm with children words ending with *–nk, –sk,* or *–st.* List the words on chart paper and encourage volunteers to make sentences using one or more of the words. Write children's sentences on chart paper and have the class read them together.

11

Summer Camp

Please send me to summer camp,
Summer camp, summer camp.
Please send me to summer camp.
My best friend will be there.

At camp we'll play in the sand,
In the sand, in the sand.
At camp we'll play in the sand,
And jump rope every day.

12

Home Connection Your child is learning to blend the sounds the letters **–nd** and **–mp** make at the end of a word. Encourage him or her to sing "Summer Camp" with you. When you go to a store, hunt for words on signs that end with these letters. Read the words together.

♫ Sung to the tune of "Mary Had a Little Lamb"

Summer Camp

Word Works Grade One

Skill 12 Final Consonant Blends, *-nd, -mp: send, camp, friend, sand, jump*

Introduce

Listen and Talk Display Phonemic Awareness Poster 12. Play the recording of "Summer Camp" (CD track 23), and ask: *Why does the child in the song want to go to summer camp? What will the child do at camp?* Encourage children to share experiences they may have had at an after-school camp or day camp.

Sing and Chime In Play the recording and encourage children to chime in when lyrics are repeated.

Work with Sounds

Say and Identify Help children hear when two sounds are pronounced together in a word. Say the word *send* and ask: *What are the last two sounds you hear in* send? Blend the sounds together and have children echo you. Say the words to the song slowly and have children clap each time they hear a word that ends with /n/ /d/. Then repeat this activity with words ending in /m/ /p/.

Blend Help children combine sounds to form a word. Ask: *What word is* /s/ /e/ /n/ /d/? Repeat this activity with the words *band, land, pond, jump, pump, lamp, stamp, limp, romp.*

Connect Sounds to Words

Look and Blend Frame the word *send* on the poster and say: /s/ /e/ /n/ /d/. Ask children to blend the sound together and say the word. Point to each letter in the word *send* as its sound is said. Explain that the /n/ and /d/ sounds are blended and pronounced together. Repeat this activity with the words *camp, sand,* and *jump.*

Substitute Write the word *hand* on chart paper. Ask a volunteer to change the /h/ to /b/ and say the new word. Write the new word, saying each sound as you write its corresponding letter. Encourage children to make other words they know by continuing to substitute the first sound in a word for another sound. Repeat this activity using the words *send, jump,* and *lamp.* List the new words on chart paper.

Innovate

Encourage children to use the words on chart paper and make up additional lyrics to the song. Invite them to sing their new songs using CD track 24.

I'll spend time with my new friend,

My new friend, my new friend.

I'll spend time with my new friend.

We'll camp out in the yard.

We'll do handstands on the grass,

On the grass, on the grass.

We'll do handstands on the grass,

Then jump rope all day long!

12

Jane and I Skate

When Jane and I skate, we like to race
Around the lake.
When Jane and I skate, we like to race
Around the lake.
We race past our friends
Who are in the lake.
There's Nate and there's Kate
And my brother Jake.
And then after we skate,
We'll swim in the lake!

13

Home Connection Your child is learning the **long a** vowel sound. Encourage him or her to sing "Jane and I Skate" with you. When you're reading a favorite book together, hunt for words with the **long a** sound. Read the words together.

♪ Sung to the tune of "The Ants Go Marching"

Jane and I Skate

Word Works Grade One

Skill 13 Long *a* (CVCe): *Jane, skate, race, lake, Nate, Kate, Jake*

Introduce

Listen and Talk Display Phonemic Awareness Poster 13. Play the recording of "Jane and I Skate" (CD track 25), and ask: *What do the two children with helmets on like to do?* Encourage children to discuss safety precautions they take when engaging in outdoor activities, such as skating, biking, and swimming.

Chime In and Act Out Play the recording again and encourage children to chime in when they feel comfortable. Invite children to make up actions for the lyrics as they listen to the song. For example, on the words *skate* and *swim,* have them pretend to do each activity.

Work with Sounds

Say and Identify Review with children that a long vowel sound is the same as the name of the letter or vowel. Help children identify the long *a* sound in words. Ask: *What sound is the same in* Jane *and* skate? Say the words to the song slowly and have children wave once each time they hear a word with a long *a* vowel sound.

Substitute Say the word *Jake.* Then segment the word and say: /j/, *–ake.* Have children echo you. Ask a volunteer to change /j/ to /b/ and say the new word. Have children make more *–ake* words by changing the initial consonant sound in *bake.* Point out that words with the same vowel and ending sounds rhyme. Repeat this activity for words ending in *–ace, –ame, –ate,* and *–ape.*

Connect Sounds to Words

Find and Underline As you say the words to the song, track the print from left to right. Have children raise their hands when you say a word that includes the long *a* sound. Invite volunteers to underline the long *a* words on the poster. Have children read the underlined words together. Then have children sing the song and clap each time they see a long *a* word.

Add Silent *e* and Make New Words Write the word *cap* on chart paper. Say each sound and point to its corresponding letter. Have children echo you. Then add *e* to *cap* to make *cape.* Say each sound and point to its corresponding letter. Explain that in *cape* the *e* is silent, but it makes the *a* say its name. A silent *e* at the end of a word makes a short vowel become a long vowel. Repeat this activity with *can/cane; pan/pane; tap/tape;* and *fad/fade.*

Innovate

Write the following song on chart paper and share it with children using CD track 26: *When I want to change a word I know like* **can** *to* **cane**—*When I want to change a word I know like* **pan** *to* **pane,** *I'll add an* **e** *to the end of each word. It changes the meaning and what I heard. So I'll add an* **e** *to* **van** *to make it* **vane**!

13

To Grandma's House

We will go to Grandma's house.
We'll take the train on Monday.
We'll pack some clothes
And games to play.
We'll stay until next Sunday.

We all hope that it won't rain,
When we leave on Monday.
If it rains, we won't complain.
We'll still make it a fun day!

14

Home Connection Your child is learning the **long a** vowel sound made by the letters **ai** and **ay**. Encourage him or her to sing "To Grandma's House" with you. When you're reading a newspaper, challenge your child to hunt for words with one of these spelling patterns. Read the words together.

♫ Sung to the tune of "Yankee Doodle"

To Grandma's House

Word Works Grade One

Skill 14 Long *a (ai, ay): train, Monday, play, stay, Sunday, rain, complain, day*

Introduce

Listen and Talk Display Phonemic Awareness Poster 14. Play the recording of "To Grandma's House" (CD track 27), and ask: *Where are the children going? When are they going? How will they get there? How long will they stay?* Invite children to share names of places they like to visit and to tell how they get to the places.

Sing and Move Play the song and encourage children to chime in when they feel comfortable. Have a volunteer be the train engineer and lead children in a line around the classroom as the song plays.

Work with Sounds

Say and Identify Help children identify the long *a* sound. Ask: *What sound is the same in* play *and* rain? Ask children to shout hooray each time they hear the long *a* sound in the following words: *play, jump, way, complain, kick, train, Tuesday, stay, Spain, hear.*

Segment and Substitute Say the word *day.* Then segment the word and say: /d/, *–ay.* Have children echo you. Ask a volunteer to change /d/ to /m/ and say the new word. Have children make more *–ay* words by changing the initial consonant sound in *may.* Point out that words with the same vowel and ending sounds rhyme. Repeat this activity for words ending in *–ain,* such as *rain* and *gain.*

Connect Sounds to Words

Find and Read Say the words to the song, tracking the print from left to right. Have volunteers find and circle words on the poster that have *–ay.* Frame the word *play.* Break the word into its separate sounds and point to the corresponding letters. Review that a letter that says its name has a long vowel sound. Explain that the letters *a* and *y* together spell the long *a* sound. Have children break the circled words with *–ay* into their separate sounds and then read the words. Repeat this activity with words on the poster that have *–ai.*

Spell and Make a List Write *day, rain,* and *pail* on chart paper. Have children substitute beginning and ending sounds in these words for other sounds to make new words. Have volunteers say, spell, and write the new words on the chart paper.

Extend

Invite children to make up sentences using one or more of the words written on chart paper. Write the sentences on the board. Then track the print as the class reads the sentences together.

14

♫ **Sung to the tune of "She'll Be Comin' Round the Mountain"**

I Will Ride My Bike

I will ride my bike a mile
And I'll smile.
I will ride my bike a mile
And I'll smile.
I will ride my bike a mile.
I will ride for quite a while.
I will ride my bike a mile
And I'll smile!

Home Connection Your child is learning the **long i** vowel sound. Encourage him or her to sing "I Will Ride My Bike" with you. When you're reading signs in your neighborhood, challenge your child to hunt for words with the **long i** sound. Read the words together.

♪ Sung to the tune of "She'll Be Comin' Round the Mountain"

I Will Ride My Bike

Word Works Grade One

Skill 15 Long *i* (CVCe): *I, ride, bike, mile, I'll, smile, quite, while*

Introduce

Listen and Share Display Phonemic Awareness Poster 15. Play the recording of "I Will Ride My Bike" (CD track 29), and ask: *What is the child in the poster doing? How long will he ride his bike?* Invite children to share things that make them smile.

Chime In and Smile Play the recording again and encourage children to chime in when they feel comfortable. Invite children to point to themselves when they hear the words *I* and *I'll.* Encourage them to make a great big grin on the word *smile.*

Work with Sounds

Say and Identify Help children identify the long *i* sound in words. Ask: *What sound is the same in* bike *and* mile? Say the words to the song slowly and have children point to their eye each time they hear a word with a long *i* vowel sound.

Substitute Say the word *ride.* Then segment the word and say: /r/, *–ide.* Have children echo you. Ask a volunteer to change /r/ to /h/ and say the new word. Have children make more *–ide* words by changing the initial consonant sound in *hide.* Point out that words with the same vowel and ending sounds rhyme. Repeat this activity for words ending in *–ike, –ite,* and *–ile.*

Connect Sounds to Words

Find and Underline As you say the words to the song, track the print from left to right. Have children point to their eyes when you say a word that includes the long *i* sound. Invite volunteers to underline the long *i* words on the poster. Then have children sing the song and clap each time they see and hear a long *i* word.

Add Silent *e* and Make New Words Write the word *hid* on chart paper. Say each sound and point to its corresponding letter. Have children echo you. Then add *e* to *hid* to make *hide.* Say each sound and point to its corresponding letter. Explain that in *hide,* the *e* is silent, but it makes the *i* say its name. A silent *e* at the end of a word makes a short vowel become a long vowel. Repeat this activity with *rid/ride; kit/kite; bit/bite;* and *sit/site.*

Innovate

Write the following song on chart paper and share it with children using CD track 30.

I will fly my kite this morning, and I'll smile.
I will fly my kite this morning, and I'll smile.
I will fly my kite and smile. I will fly it for
a while. I will fly my kite this morning,
and I'll smile!

Then, invite children to make additional lyrics using long *i* words.

15

My Pizza Pie

I make a pizza pie.
I toss the dough up high!
I get some sauce on my new tie.
I shake my head and sigh.

16

Home Connection Your child is learning the **long i** vowel sound made by the letters **ie** and **igh**. Encourage him or her to sing "My Pizza Pie" with you. When you're reading signs in your neighborhood, challenge your child to hunt for words with one of these spelling patterns. Read the words together.

♪ Sung to the tune of "The Farmer in the Dell"

My Pizza Pie

Word Works Grade One

Skill 16 Long *i (ie, igh): pie, high, tie, sigh*

Introduce

Listen and Talk Display Phonemic Awareness Poster 16. Play the recording of "My Pizza Pie" (CD track 31), and ask: *What is the boy in the poster doing? What does he do with the dough? What happens to his new tie? What does the boy do after getting sauce on his tie?* Encourage children to tell about their favorite pizza toppings.

Act Out Help children make up actions to the song. For example, children can point to themselves on the word *I*; draw a large circle in the air on the words *pizza pie;* throw their hands in the air on the word *toss;* point to and pretend they are wearing a tie on the word *tie;* shake their head and sigh on the last line of the song.

Work with Sounds

Say and Identify Review with children that a long vowel sound is the same as the name of the letter or vowel. Help children identify the long *i* sound. Ask: *What sound is the same in* pie *and* high? Ask children to hold up five fingers each time they hear the long *i* vowel sound: *lie, tip, pan, sigh, laugh, thigh, hope, lake, vie, fit.*

Sing and Clap Play the recording and have children sing along. Have them point to their eye each time they hear a word with the long *i* vowel sound.

Connect Sounds to Words

Find and Read Say the words to the song, tracking the print from left to right. Have volunteers find and circle words on the poster that have *–ie*. Frame the word *pie*. Break the word into its separate sounds and point to the corresponding letters. Review that a letter that says its name has a long vowel sound. Explain that the letters *i* and *e* together spell the long *i* sound. Repeat this activity with words on the poster that have *–igh*.

Segment Have a volunteer break *pie* into its separate sounds, saying each sound as the class taps or counts it. Ask: *How many sounds are in* pie? (2) Have children repeat the sounds heard in *pie* and write the corresponding letters on chart paper. Point out that the spelling pattern *ie* makes the long *i* vowel sound. Repeat this activity with other *–ie* and *–igh* words.

Extend

Have children brainstorm a list of words ending with *ie* or *igh*. Encourage children to use one or more of the list words in sentences. Write the sentences on chart paper and have the class read them together.

16

♫ **Sung to the tune of "Home on the Range"**

I Saw a Mole!

Oh, I saw a mole.
He dove down in his hole.
Oh, I hope he will come out again.
I'll keep watch at the hole.
He is one tiny mole.
And I think I'll name him Tiny Ben.

Ben, the tiny mole—
He lives alone down in his hole.
I hear Ben poke around,
In his hole in the ground.
Oh, I hope he will come out again!

17

Home Connection Your child is learning the **long o** vowel sound. Encourage him or her to sing "I Saw a Mole!" with you. When you're reading a magazine, challenge your child to hunt for words with the **long o** sound. Read the words together.

I Saw a Mole!

Word Works Grade One

Skill 17 Long *o* (CVC*e*): *Oh, mole, dove, hole, hope, alone, poke*

Introduce

Listen and Talk Display Phonemic Awareness Poster 17. Play the recording of "I Saw a Mole!" (CD track 33), and ask: *What did the child see? Where is the mole now? What name does the girl give to the mole?* Encourage children to share what they know about moles, chipmunks, squirrels, or other animals that live in holes in the ground.

Listen and Hum Play the recording and have children hum along. Invite them to chime in when they feel comfortable with the lyrics.

Work with Sounds

Say and Identify Help children identify the long *o* sound in words. Ask: *What sound is the same in* mole *and* hope? Say the words to the song slowly and have children raise their arms over their heads to form a circle each time they hear a word with a long *o* vowel sound.

Substitute Say the word *mole.* Then segment the word and say: /m/, *–ole.* Have children echo you. Ask a volunteer to change /m/ to /h/ and say the new word. Have children make more *–ole* words by changing the initial consonant sound in *hole.* Point out that words with the same vowel and ending sounds rhyme. Repeat this activity for words ending in *–ope, –one,* and *–oke.*

Connect Sounds to Words

Find and Underline As you say the words to the song, track the print from left to right. Have children raise their hands when you say a word that includes the long *o* sound. Invite volunteers to underline the long *o* words on the poster. Have children read the underlined words together. Then have children sing the song and clap each time they see and hear a word with a long *o* sound.

Add Silent *e* and Make New Words Write the word *hop* on chart paper. Say each sound and point to its corresponding letter. Have children echo you. Then add *e* to *hop* to make *hope.* Again, say each sound and point to its corresponding letter. Explain that in *hope* the *e* is silent, but it makes the *o* say its name. A silent *e* at the end of a word makes a short vowel become a long vowel. Repeat this activity with *cop/cope; mop/mope; glob/globe;* and *rob/robe.*

Extend

Write the word families *–ole, –ope, –one,* and *–oke* on chart paper. Have children add consonant sounds to the beginning of the word families to make long *o* words. Invite children to make up sentences using one or more of the words. Write the sentences on chart paper. Then track the print from left to right as the class reads the sentences together.

17

♫ **Sung to the tune of "My Bonnie Lies Over the Ocean"**

We See a Toad!

When Joan and I sit in our rowboat
We see a slow toad by the road.
He croaks and he hops once an hour.
We know he's one very slow toad!

Croak, hop, croak, hop,
We know he's one very slow toad, slow toad!
Croak, hop, croak, hop,
We know he's one very slow toad!

18

Home Connection Your child is learning the **long o** vowel sound made by the letters **oa** and **ow**. Encourage him or her to sing "We See a Toad!" with you. When you're reading a favorite book, challenge your child to hunt for words with one of these spelling patterns. Read the words together.

We See a Toad!

Word Works Grade One

Skill 18 Long *o* (*oa, ow*): *Joan, rowboat, slow, toad, road, croaks, know, croak*

Introduce

Listen and Talk Display Phonemic Awareness Poster 18. Play the recording of "We See a Toad!" (CD track 35), and ask: *Where are the children sitting? What do they see? What does the toad do once an hour?* Invite children to share experiences they may have had with toads or frogs.

Croak and Hop Play the recording and have children hum along. Invite them to croak or hop once in place when they hear the words *croak* and *hop* in the song.

Work with Sounds

Say and Identify Help children identify the long *o* sound. Ask: *What sound is the same in* row *and* boat? Ask children to form a circle with their thumb and index finger each time they hear the long *o* vowel sound: *row, boat, now, bath, road, Joan, slow, cape, toad, once.*

Sing and Clap Play the recording and have children sing along. Have them raise their arms over their head to form a circle each time they hear a word with the long *o* vowel sound.

Connect Sounds to Words

Find and Read Say the words to the song, tracking the print from left to right. Have volunteers find and circle words on the poster that have the *oa* spelling pattern. Frame the word *toad.* Break the word into its separate sounds and point to the corresponding letters. Explain that the letters *o* and *a* together spell the long *o* sound. Have children break the other circled words with *oa* into their separate sounds and then read the words. Repeat this activity with words on the poster that have the *ow* spelling pattern.

Spell and Make a List Write *row* and *boat* on chart paper. Have children substitute beginning and ending sounds in these words for other sounds to make new words. Have volunteers say, spell, and write the new words on the chart paper.

Extend

Using the words on chart paper, invite children to make up sentences. Write the sentences on chart paper. Then track the print from left to right as the class reads the sentences together.

♫ **Sung to the tune of "Twinkle, Twinkle, Little Star"**

My Book Is So Good!

Take a look at my new book.
I will read it by the brook.
My friend Kim says, "It's so good!"
He lives in my neighborhood.
If I read all afternoon,
I will finish very soon.

19

Home Connection Your child is learning the sounds of **oo** as in **book** and **moon**. Encourage him or her to sing "My Book Is So Good!" with you. When you're reading a newspaper together, challenge your child to hunt for words that include the **oo** spelling pattern. Read the words together.

My Book Is So Good!

Word Works Grade One

Skill 19 The Sounds of *oo* in *book* and *moon:*

look, book, brook, good, neighborhood, afternoon, soon

Introduce

Listen and Talk Display Phonemic Awareness Poster 19. Play the recording of "My Book Is So Good!" (CD track 37), and ask: *What does the girl want the boy to do? Where are the children when they are reading? What does the girl plan on doing all afternoon?* Encourage children to talk about their favorite places to read books.

Listen and Chime In Play the recording and encourage children to chime in when they feel comfortable with the lyrics. Invite children to tap out the rhythm as the song plays.

Work with Sounds

Say and Identify Help children hear and identify the sound of *oo* as in *book*. Say: /b/ /ü/ /k/ and have children echo you. Have children blend the sounds together and say the word. Repeat this activity with the words *good, cook, look, wood,* and *hood*. Play the recording and have children clap when they hear the sound of *oo* as in *book*.

Do It Again Help children hear and identify the sound of *oo* as in *soon*. Say: /s/ /ü/ /n/ and have children echo you. Have children blend the sounds together and say the word. Repeat this activity with the words *moon, noon, broom, tool, moo,* and *loop*. Play the recording and have children clap when they hear the sound of *oo* as in *soon*.

Connect Sounds to Words

Find and Read Say the words to the song, tracking the print from left to right. Have volunteers find and circle words on the poster that have *oo*. Frame the word *book*. Break the word into its separate sounds and point to the corresponding letters. Explain that in the word *book, oo* spells the /ü/ sound. Then frame and separate the sounds in *soon*. Explain that in the word *soon, oo* spells the /ü/ sound. Repeat this activity for each circled word on the poster.

Substitute Write *book* on chart paper. Invite children to change the /b/ to other sounds they know to make words that rhyme with *book*. Point out that rhyming words have the same vowel and ending sounds. Repeat this activity with the words *good, soon, loop, boom, food,* and *tool*.

Extend

Invite children to use the words on the chart paper to make up sentences. Write the sentences on the board. Then track the print from left to right as the class reads the sentences together.

19

June Plays a Tune

June likes to play a tune on her flute,
A tune on her flute, a tune on her flute.
June likes to play a tune on her flute.
June is sure to please us!

Home Connection Your child is learning the **long u** sound. Encourage him or her to sing "June Plays a Tune" with you. When you're reading a magazine, challenge your child to hunt for words with the **long u** sound. Read the words together.

June Plays a Tune

Word Works Grade One

Skill 20 Long *u* (CVC*e*): *June, tune, flute*

Introduce

Listen and Talk Display Phonemic Awareness Poster 20. Play the recording of "June Plays a Tune" (CD track 39), and ask: *What does June like to do?* Invite children to talk about things they like to do that make others happy.

Chime In and Sing Play the recording and have children chime in when they feel comfortable. Encourage children to pretend they are playing flutes as they listen to the song.

Work with Sounds

Say and Identify Help children identify the long *u* sound in words. Ask: *What sound is the same in* June *and* tune? Say the words to the song slowly and have children clap each time they hear a word with a long *u* vowel sound.

Categorize Help children recognize words with long *u* sounds. Ask: *What word doesn't have a long* u *vowel sound? June, tune, cape.* Repeat the activity with these sets of words: *huge/fun/cube; cut/cute/mule;* and *fuse/put/dune.*

Connect Sounds to Words

Read and Find Say the words to the song, tracking the print from left to right. Have children raise their hands or whistle when you say a word that includes the long *u* sound. Invite volunteers to underline the long *u* words on the poster. Have children read the underlined words together. Then have children sing the song and clap each time they see and hear a word with a long *u* sound.

Add Silent *e* and Make New Words Write the word *cut* on chart paper. Say each sound and point to its corresponding letter. Have children echo you. Then add *e* to *cut* to make *cute.* Again, say each sound and point to its corresponding letter. Explain that in *cute* the *e* is silent, but it makes the *u* say its name. A silent *e* at the end of a word makes a short vowel become a long vowel. Repeat this activity with *hug/huge* and *cub/cube.*

Extend

Have children change the vowel sound in a word to the long *u* sound to make a new word. Use the word pairs *coat/cute; foam/fume; mole/mule; cab/cube; ton/tune; Jane/June;* and *fizz/fuse.*

20

♫ **Sung to the tune of "This Old Man"**

I'm as Happy as Can Be!

This is me. This is Eve.
This is our new neighbor Steve.
When we play jump rope,
They turn the rope for me.
I'm as happy as can be!

Home Connection Your child is learning the **long e** sound. Encourage him or her to sing "I'm as Happy as Can Be!" with you. When you're reading a favorite book together, challenge your child to hunt for words with the **long e** sound. Read the words together.

I'm as Happy as Can Be!

Word Works Grade One

Skill 21 Long *e: me, Eve, Steve, we, be*

Introduce

Listen and Talk Display Phonemic Awareness Poster 21. Play the recording of "I'm as Happy as Can Be!" (CD track 41), and ask: *How many children are pictured on the poster? What are the children playing?* Invite children to tell about activities they do with their friends that make them happy.

Act Out Play the recording. Have children act out the song by pointing to themselves on the words *me* and *I'm* and pointing to a classmate on the words *Eve, Steve,* and *we.* As children listen to lines three and four, they can pretend to jump rope in place. Encourage them to smile at the end of the song.

Work with Sounds

Say and Identify Help children identify the long *e* sound in words. Ask: *What sound is the same in* me *and* Eve? Say the words to the song slowly and have children point to themselves each time they hear a word with a long *e* vowel sound. Acknowledge the word *happy* as having a long *e* sound.

Categorize Help children recognize words with long *e* sounds. Ask: *What word doesn't have a long* e *sound*—me, by, be? Repeat the activity with these sets of words: *Steve/seam/set; at/meat/bead;* and *tree/way/peach.*

Segment Have a volunteer break *me* into its separate sounds, saying each sound as the class taps or counts it. Ask: *How many sounds are in me?* Have children repeat the sounds heard in *me* and write the corresponding letters on chart paper. Explain that when *e* is the only vowel in a word and it's at the end of the word, it says its name. Repeat the activity with *Steve*. Explain that when *e* is at the end of a word that has another vowel in it, the ending *e* is silent and makes the first vowel long.

Connect Sounds to Words

Read and Find Say the words to the song, tracking the print from left to right. Have children clap when you say a word that includes the long *e* sound. Invite volunteers to underline the long *e* words on the poster. Have children read the underlined words together. If *happy* is underlined, explain that the letter *y* spells the long *e* sound. Then have children sing the song and clap each time they see and hear a long *e* word.

Innovate

Invite children to substitute names that rhyme or end the same for the names *Eve* and *Steve* in the song, such as *Ted/Fred, Jan/Dan, Jen/Ben,* and *Kate/Nate.* Play CD track 42 and have children sing the song with new names.

21

♫ Sung to the tune of "Mary Had a Little Lamb"

The Best Team!

Come see our team play this week,
Play this week, play this week.
Come see our team play this week.
I will save you a seat!

We're the team that can't be beat,
Can't be beat, can't be beat.
We're the team that can't be beat.
I think that you'll agree!

22

Home Connection Your child is learning the **long e** vowel sound made by the letters **ea** and **ee**. Encourage him or her to sing "The Best Team!" with you. When you go shopping, challenge your child to hunt for words on signs and products with one of these spelling patterns. Read the words together.

The Best Team!

Word Works Grade One

Skill 22 Long *e (ee, ea): see, team, week, seat, beat, agree*

Introduce

Listen and Talk Display Phonemic Awareness Poster 22. Play the recording of "The Best Team!" (CD track 43), and ask: *What is the song asking you to do? When will the team play?* Invite children to share experiences they have had playing on a team.

Chime In and Act Out Play the recording and encourage children to chime in on the repeated lyrics. Invite children to bounce a pretend basketball in time with the music. Suggest they "take a shot at the basket" on the words *seat* and *agree.*

Work with Sounds

Listen and Identify Help children identify the long *e* sound in words. Ask: *What sound is the same in* team *and* week? Say the words to the song slowly and have children pretend to beat a drum each time they hear a word with a long *e* sound.

Substitute Have children change the vowel sound in a word to the long *e* sound to make a new word. Use the word pairs *book/beak; mat/meat; Tom/team; grain/green; fed/feed;* and *tray/tree.*

Connect Sounds to Words

Find and Read Say the words to the song, tracking the print from left to right. Have volunteers find and circle words on the poster that have the *ea* spelling pattern. Frame the word *team.* Break the word into its separate sounds and point to the corresponding letters. Explain that the letters *e* and *a* together spell the long *e* sound. Have children break the other circled words with *ea* into their separate sounds and read the words. Repeat this activity with words on the poster that have the *ee* spelling pattern.

Spell and Write Choose three or four of the following rimes and write them on chart paper: *-each, -ead, –eak, -eal, -ean, -eat, -ee, -eed, -ee, -eel, -eem, -eet, -eeze.* Have volunteers pick a rime, add an initial consonant sound and write the words on the chart paper. As children write their words, encourage them to say each sound as they write the corresponding letter or letters. Have the class read the words together.

Extend

Invite children to use one or more of the words on chart paper in sentences. Write the sentences on the board and have children read them together.

22

Bucky, My Pup

Bucky is my happy pup.
He's tiny and he's furry.
He runs right by me, out the door.
He's always in a hurry!

Bucky runs outside to play.
He is very funny.
He will spy on my friend's cat
Who comes out when it's sunny!

23

Home Connection Your child is learning the sound that the letter **y** makes at the end of a word. Encourage him or her to sing "Bucky, My Pup" with you. When you're reading a magazine, challenge your child to hunt for words that end in **y**. Read the words together.

Bucky, My Pup

Word Works Grade One

Skill 23 Words with *y (long i, long e):*

Bucky, my, happy, tiny, furry, by, hurry, very, funny, spy, sunny

Introduce

Listen and Talk Display Phonemic Awareness Poster 23. Play the recording of "Bucky, My Pup" (CD track 45), and ask: *What is the name of the puppy? What does he look like? What does he like to do?* Invite children to discuss what their pets like to do. To help children learn the words to the song, have them make up actions for each line.

Work with Sounds

Listen and Identify Say the words to the song slowly, asking children to listen for the long *e* sound at the end of words. Then ask them to raise their arms in a circle when they hear long *e* at the end of a word. Say the words to the song again and have them identify words that end with the long *i* sound.

Categorize Help children recognize words with the long *e* sound at the end. Ask: *What word doesn't have a long* e *sound as the last sound*—funny, monkey, sky? *What vowel sound do you hear at the end of* sky? Repeat the activity with these sets of words: *shy/happy/penny; very/by/baby; tricky/dry/cloudy;* and *sunny/tiny/my.*

Connect Sounds to Words

Find and Read Say the words to the song, tracking the print from left to right. Have volunteers find and circle words on the poster that end in *y*. Frame and say each circled word and have children echo you. Ask children what the last sound is in each word. Point out that the long *e* or long *i* vowel sound at the end of the word is spelled with a *y*.

Write and Clap Make two columns on chart paper and write *happy* at the top of one column and *my* at the top of the other column. Say each word and have children echo you. Ask children what the last sound is in each word. Return to the circled words on the poster and have children say each word and tell what the last sound in the word is. Write the word in the correct column. Then repeat each word in the columns and have children clap the syllables with you. Help children discover that in words with one syllable, the ending *y* has a long *i* sound, and in words with two syllables, the ending *y* has a long *e* sound. Encourage children to add other words they know to the columns.

23

♫ Sung to the tune of "Are You Sleeping, Brother John?"

Shane Got Sea Shells!

Shane got sea shells.
Shane got sea shells
At the shore, at the shore.
Shane saw fish go splish, splash.
Shane saw fish go splish, splash
At the shore, at the shore.

24

Home Connection Your child is learning the sound of **sh** as in **shell** and **fish**. Encourage him or her to sing "Shane Got Sea Shells!" with you. When you go to the grocery store, challenge your child to find words that begin or end with the letters **sh**. Read the words together.

Shane Got Sea Shells!

Word Works Grade One

Skill 24 Initial and Final Digraph, *sh: Shane, shells, shore, fish, splish, splash*

Introduce

Listen and Share Display Phonemic Awareness Poster 24. Play the recording of "Shane Got Sea Shells!" (CD track 47), and ask: *What did Shane get? What did Shane see? Where is Shane?* Encourage children to tell about things they collect.

Listen and Tap Play the recording and have children tap along in time to the music. Encourage them to chime in on the repeated lyrics.

Work with Sounds

Listen and Identify Help children hear the /sh/ sound at the beginning or end of words. Say: /sh/-/sh/-/sh/ and have children echo you. Ask: *What sound is the same in* dish *and* shop? *What part of* dish *has the /sh/ sound? What part of* shop *has the /sh/ sound?* Repeat this activity using these words: *shape, ship, smash, shirt, squish,* and *flush.*

Listen and Shush Play the recording and ask children to put their fingers to their lips and make a shushing sound when they hear a word that begins or ends with /sh/. Play the song again and encourage children to chime in and sing the repeated lyrics.

Connect Sounds to Words

Find and Read Say the words to the song, tracking the print from left to right. Have volunteers find and circle words on the poster that have the spelling pattern *sh*. Frame the word *Shane*. Break the word into its separate sounds and point to the corresponding letters. Explain that the letters *s* and *h* are used together to stand for a single sound. Review the role silent *e* plays in word spellings. Repeat this activity with other circled words on the poster.

Substitute and Write New Words Using magnetic letters on a cookie sheet, spell the word *tip*. Have children break the word into its separate sounds as you point to the corresponding letters. Ask a volunteer to change the /t/ to /sh/ and read the new word. Repeat the activity with these word pairs: *cape/shape; mop/shop; dirt/shirt; care/share; bark/shark;* and *lock/shock*. Extend the activity by changing ending sounds in words to /sh/: *mat/mash; flap/flash; rat/rash; cat/cash; dip/dish;* and *fit/fish.*

Innovate

Brainstorm with children words that begin or end with *sh* and make a list on chart paper. Encourage children to write new lyrics for the song. Have them sing their songs using CD track 48. For example: *She saw big ships; She saw big ships; At the shore, At the shore; Then she saw a big shark; Then she saw a big shark, With sharp teeth, With sharp teeth!*

24

Theo's Tooth

Theo had a tooth pulled out today.
His mouth is sore so he can't play.
I bring Theo chicken broth at noon.
I think that he'll feel better soon!

Home Connection Your child is learning the sound of **th** as in **think** and **tooth**. Encourage him or her to sing "Theo's Tooth" with you. When you read a newspaper together, challenge your child to find words that begin or end with the letters **th**. Read the words together.

Theo's Tooth

Word Works Grade One

Skill 25 Initial and Final Digraph, *th: Theo, tooth, mouth, broth, think, that*

Introduce

Listen and Talk Display Phonemic Awareness Poster 25. Play the recording of "Theo's Tooth" (CD track 49), and ask: *What happened to Theo today? What did Theo's friend bring him at noon?* Invite children to share experiences about family members or friends bringing them something to make them feel better.

Listen and Hum Play the recording and have children hum along. Invite them to chime in when they feel comfortable with the lyrics.

Work with Sounds

Listen and Identify Help children hear the /th/ sound at the beginning or end of words. Say: /th/-/th/-/th/ and have children echo you. Ask: *What sound is the same in* think *and* mouth? *What part of* think *has the* /th/ *sound? What part of* mouth *has the* /th/ *sound?* Repeat this activity using these words: *thumb, thimble, broth, thank, south,* and *with.*

Listen and Clap Play the recording and ask children to clap when they hear a word that begins or ends with /th/. Play the song again and encourage children to sing the words that have the /th/ sound.

Connect Sounds to Words

Find and Read Say the words to the song, tracking the print from left to right. Have volunteers find and circle words on the poster that have the spelling pattern *th.* Frame the word *Theo.* Break the word into its separate sounds and point to the corresponding letters. Explain that the letters *t* and *h* are used together to stand for a single sound. Repeat this activity with other circled words on the poster.

Substitute and Write New Words Using magnetic letters on a cookie sheet, spell the word *sink.* Have children break the word into its separate sounds as you point to the corresponding letters. Ask a volunteer to change the /s/ to /th/ and read the new word. Repeat the activity with these word pairs: *numb/thumb; born/thorn; nimble/thimble; bump/thump;* and *bought/thought.* Extend the activity by changing ending sounds in words to /th/: *toot/tooth; pad/path; bag/bath;* and *teem/teeth.*

Extend

Brainstorm with children words they know that either begin or end with *th.* Write the words on chart paper. Have children blend the separate sounds together and read each word.

25

♫ Sung to the tune of "Home on the Range"

I See a Gray Whale

I see a gray whale with a white spotted tail,
And I whistle when he swims by me.
While I whistle at him, he continues to swim.
Oh, I wish the whale would look at me!

I see a gray whale.
The whale has a white spotted tail.
While I whistle at him, he continues to swim.
Oh, I wish the whale would look at me!

26

Home Connection Your child is learning the sound of **wh** as in **whale** and **white**. Encourage him or her to sing "I See a Gray Whale" with you. When you read a magazine together, challenge your child to find words that begin with the letters **wh**. Read the words together.

I See a Gray Whale

Word Works Grade One

Skill 26 Initial Digraph, *wh: whale, white, whistle, when, while*

Introduce

Listen and Share Display Phonemic Awareness Poster 26. Play the recording of "I See a Gray Whale" (CD track 51), and *ask: What does the child see? What happened when the child whistled? What does the child want the whale to do?* Invite children to share experiences about animals they have seen.

Act Out Play the recording and encourage children to chime in when they feel comfortable. To help children learn the words to the song, have them point to themselves on the word *I;* whistle on the word *whistle;* make a swimming stroke on the word *swim;* point to their eyes on the word *look;* and point to themselves on the word *me.*

Work with Sounds

Listen and Identify Help children hear the /hw/ sound at the beginning of a word. Say /hw/-/hw/-/hw/ and have children echo you. Ask: *What sound do you hear at the beginning of* whale *and* white? Repeat this activity using these words: *whistle, when, while, wheel, wheat, whirl,* and *why.*

Listen and Whistle Play the recording and ask children to whistle when they hear a word that begins with /hw/. If children are unable to whistle, suggest that they wave. Play the song again and encourage children to sing the words that begin with /hw/.

Connect Sounds to Words

Find and Read Say the words to the song, tracking the print from left to right. Have volunteers find and circle words on the poster that begin with the spelling pattern *wh.* Frame the word *whale.* Break the word into its separate sounds and point to the corresponding letters. Explain that the letters *w* and *h* are used together to stand for a single sound. Repeat this activity with other circled words on the poster.

Substitute and Write New Words Using magnetic letters on a cookie sheet, spell the word *pen.* Have children break the word into its separate sounds as you point to the corresponding letters. Ask a volunteer to change the /p/ to /hw/ and read the new word. Repeat the activity with these word pairs: *bright/white; pale/whale; thistle/whistle; mile/while; sip/whip; peel/wheel; meat/wheat;* and *my/why.*

Extend

Brainstorm with children words they know that begin with *wh.* Write the words on chart paper. Challenge children to use one or more of the words in sentences. Write their sentences on the board and have children read them with you.

26

♫ **Sung to the tune of "I've Been Working on the Railroad"**

Chowder for Lunch!

Watch me stir my chicken chowder.
I add cheddar cheese.
Watch me stir my chicken chowder.
My chowder's sure to please!
Watch me make a batch of peach tarts.
What a tasty lunch.
Later, we'll chat on my big porch
While we munch and munch!

27

Home Connection Your child is learning the sound of **ch** and **tch** as in **chicken**, **peach**, and **watch**. Encourage him or her to sing "Chowder for Lunch!" with you. When you read a favorite book together, challenge your child to find words with the letters **ch** or **tch**. Read the words together.

Chowder for Lunch!

Word Works Grade One

Skill 27 Initial and Final Digraphs, *ch, tch: watch, chicken, chowder, cheddar, cheese, batch, peach, lunch, chat, porch, munch*

Introduce

Listen and Talk Display Phonemic Awareness Poster 27. Play the recording of "Chowder for Lunch!" (CD track 53), and ask: *What kind of chowder is the boy stirring? What does the child add to the chowder? What else is the boy making for lunch? Where will the boy and his mom eat lunch?* Invite children to tell about foods they make with the help of an adult.

Act Out Play the recording and encourage children to chime in when they feel comfortable. To help children learn the words to the song, have them make up actions for the words: *watch, me, stir, add, please, tasty, chat,* and *munch.*

Work with Sounds

Listen and Identify Help children hear the /ch/ sound at the beginning or end of words. Say /ch/-/ch/-/ch/ and have children echo you. Ask: *What sound is the same in* chicken *and* watch? *What part of* chicken *has the /ch/ sound? What part of* watch *has the /ch/ sound?* Repeat this activity using these words: *chair, cheer, pitch, chin, catch,* and *beach.*

Listen and Touch Your Chin Play the recording and ask children to touch their chins when they hear a word that begins or ends with /ch/. Play the song again and encourage children to sing the words that have the /ch/ sound.

Connect Sounds to Words

Find and Read Say the words to the song, tracking the print from left to right. Have volunteers find and circle words on the poster that have the spelling pattern *ch* or *tch.* Frame the word *chicken.* Break the word into its separate sounds and point to the corresponding letters. Explain that the letters *c* and *h* are used together to stand for a single sound. Next, frame the word *lunch,* segment the sounds, and discuss the /ch/ sound at the end of the word. Finally, frame the word *watch* and segment the sounds. Help children discover that the letters *tch* are used together to stand for the /ch/ sound.

Delete Write the word *ditch* on chart paper. Ask: *If you take away the /d/ in* ditch, *what word do you have?* Invite a volunteer to write the word *itch* next to *ditch.* Repeat this activity with the words *couch/ouch; beach/each; chin/in; chat/at;* and *chair/air.*

27

Norm and Marge

When Norm and his friend, Marge
Play horn and guitar,
Everyone thinks that
Each one is a star!

They'll play at a party
Or in our town's park.
They play for the people
Until it gets dark.

Home Connection Your child is learning the sound of **ar** and **or** as in **horn** and **guitar**. Encourage him or her to sing "Norm and Marge" with you. When you read a newspaper together, challenge your child to find words with the letters **ar** or **or**. Read the words together.

Norm and Marge

Skill 28 *r*-Controlled Vowels, *ar, or: Norm, Marge, horn, guitar, star, party, park, dark*

Introduce

Listen and Talk Display Phonemic Awareness Poster 28. Play the recording of "Norm and Marge" (CD track 55), and ask: *Who is Norm's friend? What musical instruments do they play? Where do they play their instruments? When do they stop playing?* Invite children to tell about musical instruments they know how to play or would like to learn to play.

Be a Star! Play the recording and encourage children to pretend to play either horn or guitar along with the music. Invite children to chime in on the lyrics when they feel comfortable.

Work with Sounds

Listen and Identify Help children hear the /är/ sound in words. Say: /är/ /är/ /är/ and have children echo you. Ask: *What sound is the same in* Marge *and* star? Play the recording and have children raise their hands each time they hear a word with /är/. Continue the activity and say: /ȯr/-/ȯr/-/ȯr/ and have children echo you. Ask: *What sound is the same in* Norm *and* horn? Play the recording again and have children clap each time they hear a word with /ȯr/.

Add Have children make new words by adding a sound to the beginning of the word *ark*. Ask: *What word do you have if you add /p/ to the beginning of* ark? Invite children to add other sounds to *ark* to make new words. Repeat this activity with the words *art* and *arm.*

Substitute Say the word *born.* Then segment the word by saying: /b/ /ȯr/ /n/. Have children echo you. Ask a volunteer to change /b/ to /k/ and say the new word. Have children continue substituting initial consonant sounds to make new words. Extend the activity by changing the initial consonant sounds in *cork* and *port.*

Connect Sounds to Words

Find and Read Say the words to the song, tracking the print from left to right. Have volunteers find and circle words on the poster that have the spelling pattern *ar.* Frame the word *star.* Break the word into its separate sounds and point to the corresponding letters. Explain that when *r* follows a vowel, the vowel has neither a long nor a short sound. Repeat this activity with other circled words on the poster. Extend the activity for words on the poster with the spelling pattern *or.*

Substitute On chart paper, write the following words in columns: *car, dark, farm,* and *cart.* Ask volunteers to substitute the first letter with another letter or letters and say and spell the new words. Write the words in the correct column. Have children read the words together. Repeat this activity with *Norm, born, cork,* and *sort.*

28

♫ **Sung to the tune of "Hush, Little Baby"**

I Spy

I spy a boy buying one blue shirt.
I spy a girl buying one red skirt.
I spy a clerk helping them today.
I spy the mother. She will pay.
She has the money in her purse.
She pays the clerk. She is a nurse!

29

Home Connection Your child is learning the sound of **er**, **ir**, and **ur** as in **clerk**, **shirt**, and **nurse**. Encourage him or her to sing "I Spy" with you. When you read a favorite book together, challenge your child to find words with the letters **er**, **ir**, or **ur**. Read the words together.

I Spy

Word Works Grade One

Skill 29 *r*-Controlled Vowels, *er, ir, ur: shirt, girl, skirt, clerk, mother, purse, nurse*

Introduce

Listen and Talk Display Phonemic Awareness Poster 29. Play the recording of "I Spy" (CD track 57), and ask: *What is the boy doing? What is the girl doing? What is the clerk doing? What is the mother doing?* Encourage children to talk about shopping experiences they have had.

Listen and Act Out Play the recording and invite children to chime in when they feel comfortable. Encourage them to act out some of the words to help them learn the lyrics. Children can point to their eyes on the words *I spy,* point to a shirt or skirt on lines 1 and 2, and pretend to take money out of a purse and pay the clerk on lines 5 and 6.

Work with Sounds

Listen and Identify Help children hear the /ər/ sound in words. Say /ər/-/ər/-/ər/ and have children echo you. Ask: *What sound is the same in* shirt, clerk, *and* purse? Play the recording and have children point to their eye each time they hear a word with /ər/.

Blend Have children combine sounds to form words. Ask: *What word is /sh/ /ər/ /t/?* Continue this activity by using these words: *bird, curl, girl, fur, her, nerve, burn, fern, herd, perch,* and *burst.*

Connect Sounds to Words

Listen and Underline Say the words to the song, tracking the print from left to right. Have volunteers underline words on the poster that have the /ər/ sound in the middle. Frame each word and say its separate sounds, pointing to the corresponding letters. Draw a box around *er, ir,* or *ur* as you say /ər/. Explain that the letters *ir, er,* and *ur* spell the same vowel sound. Have children read the underlined words together.

List and Write Sentences Write *er, ir,* and *ur* in three columns on chart paper. List the words from the poster that contain these spelling patterns in the appropriate column. Have children brainstorm other words they know with the same vowel sound and list them in the columns. Invite volunteers to use one or more of the words in sentences. Write the sentences on the board and have children read them together.

Innovate

Invite children to create new lyrics to the song by completing the sentence *I spy . . .* Encourage them to sing their lyrics using CD track 58.

I spy a bird perching in a tree.

I spy a purse that belongs to me.

29

Roy and Joy's Party

Join Roy. He's having a party.
Join Joy. She's having a party.
Oh, boy! We're having a party.
Join us and enjoy the fun!

Join Roy. He sings and makes noise now.
Join Joy. She sings and makes noise now.
Oh, boy! We'll sing and make noise now.
Join us and enjoy the fun!

30

Home Connection Your child is learning the sound of **oi** and **oy** as in **join** and **boy**. Encourage him or her to sing "Roy and Joy's Party" with you. When you read a magazine together, challenge your child to find words with the letters **oi** and **oy**. Read the words together.

Roy and Joy's Party

Word Works Grade One

Skill 30 Diphthongs, *oi*, *oy*: *join, Roy, Joy, boy, enjoy, noise*

Introduce

Listen and Talk Display Phonemic Awareness Poster 30. Play the recording of "Roy and Joy's Party" (CD track 59), and ask: *What are Roy and Joy doing? What will the children do at the party?* Invite children to share the kinds of activities they like to do at parties.

Chime In and Enjoy Play the recording and invite children to chime in and sing when they feel comfortable. Divide the class into two groups. Have one group wave their hands in the air while the other group sings lines 1 and 5 about Roy. Reverse roles on lines 2 and 6 about Joy. Have the two groups sing the other lines of the song together.

Work with Sounds

Listen and Identify Help children hear the /ȯi/ sound in words. Say /ȯi/-/ȯi/-/ȯi/ and have children echo you. Ask: *What sound is the same in* join *and* Roy? Play the recording and have children join their hands over their heads each time they hear a word with /ȯi/.

Substitute Have children change the vowel sound they hear in a word to /ȯi/ to make a new word. Say: *The word is* by. *Change the* long i *sound to /ȯi/. What's the new word?* Continue this activity with *paint/point; jay/Joy; jean/join; news/noise; vase/voice; seal/soil; cone/coin;* and *tea/toy.*

Connect Sounds to Words

Listen and Underline Say the words to the song, tracking the print from left to right. Have volunteers underline words on the poster that have the /ȯi/ sound. Frame each word and say its separate sounds, pointing to the corresponding letters. Draw a box around *oi* or *oy* as you say /ȯi/. Explain that the letters *oi* or *oy* together spell the vowel sound /ȯi/. Have children read the underlined words together.

List and Write Sentences Write *oi* and *oy* in two columns on chart paper. List the words from the poster that contain these spelling patterns in the appropriate column. Have children brainstorm other words they know with the same vowel sound and list them in the columns. Invite volunteers to use one or more of the words in sentences. Write the sentences on the board and have children read them together.

Innovate

Invite children to make up their own lyrics using words with *oi* and *oy*. Encourage children to sing their new songs, using CD track 60. For example: *Joy's dad will broil a chicken; Joy's dad will broil a chicken; Joy's dad will broil a chicken; Let's eat and enjoy ourselves!*

30

♫ Sung to the tune of "Rockabye, Baby"

Count the Clouds

Count all the clouds.
Please count them right now.
Then find the cloud
That's shaped like a cow.
When you have found
The cow in the sky,
Then point out the owl cloud
Floating nearby!

Home Connection Your child is learning the sound of **ou** and **ow** as in **clouds** and **cow.** Encourage him or her to sing "Count the Clouds" with you. When you read a book together, challenge your child to find words with the letters **ou** or **ow.** Read the words together.

Count the Clouds

Word Works Grade One

Skill 31 Diphthongs, *ou, ow: count, clouds, now, cloud, cow, found, out, owl*

Introduce

Listen and Talk Display Phonemic Awareness Poster 31. Play the recording of "Count the Clouds" (CD track 61), and ask: *How many clouds are there on the poster? (9) What are the clouds shaped like?* Invite children to share what they see when they look up at the sky.

Work with Sounds

Listen and Identify Help children hear the /aü/ sound in words. Say /aü/-/aü/-/aü/ and have children echo you. Ask: *What sound is the same in* count *and* owl? Play the recording and have children clap each time they hear a word with /aü/. Tell children that this sound can be at the beginning, middle, or end of a word.

Add Have children add a sound to the beginning of *out* to make words that rhyme, or have the same vowel and ending sounds. *(about, doubt, pout, route, clout, spout)*

Substitute Have children change the vowel sound they hear in a word to /aü/ to make a new word. Say: *The word is* tan. *Change /a/ to /aü/. What's the new word?* Continue this activity with *new/now; key/cow; lid/loud; brain/brown; spot/spout;* and *find/found.*

Connect Sounds to Words

Listen and Underline Say the words to the song, tracking the print from left to right. Have volunteers underline words on the poster that have the /aü/ sound. Frame each word and say its separate sounds, pointing to the corresponding letters. Draw a box around *ou* or *ow* as you say /aü/. Explain that the letters *ou* or *ow* together spell the vowel sound /aü/. Have children read the underlined words together.

List and Write Sentences Write *cloud, pout, found, now,* and *down* on chart paper. Have children change the beginning sounds in the words to make as many rhyming words as they can. Write the words in the appropriate columns. Invite volunteers to use one or more of the words in sentences. Write the sentences on the board and have children read them together.

Extend

Have children remove a sound from a word to make new words. Ask: *What is* howl *without the* /h/? Continue this activity with *spout/pout; pout/out; ground/round;* and *cloud/loud.*

31

I Saw Paul

I saw Paul do somersaults,
Somersaults, somersaults.
I saw Paul do somersaults.
He taught me what to do.

I did cartwheels on the lawn,
On the lawn, on the lawn.
I did cartwheels on the lawn.
Paul saw me do them, too!

Home Connection Your child is learning the sound of **au** and **aw** as in **Paul** and **saw**. Encourage him or her to sing "I Saw Paul" with you. When you look at a magazine together, challenge your child to find words with the letters **au** or **aw**.

I Saw Paul

Skill 32 Vowel Patterns, *au, aw: saw, Paul, somersaults, taught, lawn*

Introduce

Listen and Talk Display Phonemic Awareness Poster 32. Play the recording of "I Saw Paul" (CD track 63), and ask: *What did the girl see Paul do? What does the girl do on the lawn?* Invite children to tell about tumbling activities they know how to do.

Chime In and Clap Play the recording and encourage children to chime in on the repeated words. Invite them to clap in time with the music as the song plays.

Work with Sounds

Listen and Identify Help children hear the /ȯ/ sound in words. Say /ȯ/-/ȯ/-/ȯ/ and have children echo you. Ask: *What sound is the same in* saw *and* Paul? Play the recording and have children pretend to yawn each time they hear a word with /ȯ/.

Substitute Have children change the vowel sound they hear in a word to /ȯ/ to make a new word. Say: *The word is* line. *Change the long* i *to* /ȯ/. *What's the new word?* Continue this activity with *felt/fault; dry/draw; sea/saw; heel/haul; fin/fawn; clue/claw; jay/jaw; pie/paw;* and *line/lawn.*

Connect Sounds to Words

Find and Clap Say the words to the song, tracking the print on the poster from left to right. Have volunteers underline words on the poster that have the /ȯ/ sound. Frame each word and say its separate sounds, pointing to the corresponding letters. Draw a box around *au* and *aw* as you say /ȯ/. Explain that the letters *au* and *aw* together spell the vowel sound /ȯ/. Have children read the underlined words together.

List and Write Sentences Write *saw, lawn,* and *Paul* on chart paper. Have children change the beginning sounds in the words to make as many rhyming words as they can. Write the words in the appropriate columns. Add other words with the vowel patterns *au* or *aw* that the children know to the list. Invite volunteers to use one or more of the words in sentences. Write the sentences on the board and have children read them together.

Innovate

Have children write new lyrics to the song, using some of the words on the chart paper. Encourage them to sing their new songs, using CD track 64. For example: *I saw Saul on his seesaw; His seesaw, his seesaw; I saw Saul on his seesaw; He played with his friend Paul!*

Teacher Notes